Laventille

To Jessica.
Thank you for your continued support.
Friendships + smiles
Enjoy
Love
Sheree
12/03/15
xxx

Laventille

Sheree Mack

Smoke
STACK
BOOKS

Smokestack Books
1 Lake Terrace, Grewelthorpe, Ripon HG4 3BU
e-mail: info@smokestack-books.co.uk
www.smokestack-books.co.uk

ISBN 978-0-9929581-2-1

Middlesbrough
moving forward

Smokestack Books is represented
by Inpress Ltd

Acknowledgements

Thanks are due to the editors who first published the following poems, sometimes in earlier versions: *The Abstraction of Verse, And Other Poems, Conversations Across Borders Project, Incmag, Mr Subtle Tea.com, Newcastles of the World, The North East Poetry Journal, Poetry Kit, Poui: the literary magazine of the University of the West Indies, Red Savina Review, Under the Radar, The White of the Moon.*

'Windrush Isle' appeared as a poemfilm as part of the Whitley Bay Film Festival Arthouses (North Tyneside) 2012. 'Clementine' was one of the poems dropped in the Rain of Poems by Casagrande Collective at Poetry Parnassus, Southbank (London) 2012.

where the inheritors of the middle
passage stewed
five to a room, still clamped below
their hatch,
breeding felonies,
whose lives revolve around prison,
graveyard, church.

Derek Walcott, 'Laventille'

Contents

Laventille Love Song

after Langston Hughes

If I could take the Laventille night
and wrap it around you,
take the electric cables,
take the chanting, screams, gun shots
and tone their harshness all the way down.

Then I would take Laventille's heartbeat,
make a steelpan whine,
put it on a record and let it spin
and while we listen to it play,
dance with you till the break of day.

The Ledger is Lost

2 August 1498

After weeks languishing in the doldrums,
we sight three peaks on land.
They meet us upon the water.
Huge men and women,
naked from the waist up.
We stay on the ship
to play a greeting on the drums.
Beating out our intentions,
softly with a skin caress.
We come in peace, we come in peace.
We smile wide, too wide.
And dance. This is not our way but theirs.
This is new found land to the West.
We want to get first impressions right.
We are fired upon. We are misunderstood.

16 August 1896

After years of tropical birds
coming home to roost,
this island is a mash up of blood.
We meet on a spectrum of skin shades;
blue black, black, brown, chestnut,
ochre, caramel, yellow, peach and white.
We are a beautiful intermingling of cultures
wearing our differences;
a chorus of necklaces
around a long slender black neck.

31 August 1969

We have lost our way.
It is as it was at the beginning
and so too at the end.
This land of our birth
is no longer a part of our being.
Our country is no longer ours.
The children follow the call
of their names to find their way home.
But who or what can call
home to rest a whole island
and its future?

Papa Bois

Arima, Chaguanas, Poole, Couva, Petit Valley, Success Village,
Rio Claro, Libertyville, Sea Lots, San Fernando, Tunapuna.

Buried deep in the forest,
is an old man of Africa
with cloven hooves, who
despite his age is strong and fast.
Protecting the fauna and flora,
if you should meet
him, greet politely.
Bonjour, vieux Papa.
He will smile at your use of patois,
the tongue that lingers
around our island, tracing
us back to something beyond.

Port of Spain, Beecham Highway, San Rafael, Morvant,
Laventille, New Grant, East Dry River, Sangre Grande, Maraval.

Maman De L'Eau

Before you notice the dead fish and rotting things;
the drowned pet amongst the rusting cans,
you will see her –
    a woman, and what a woman.

She will be amongst the shallow waters,
washing her clothes, naked
from the waist up with only her
long hair as a means of covering.

Her long flowing skirts
will skim the water's edge.
She will be singing a song in the sunlight,
a song you recognise but cannot name.

You will be drawn towards her, as she lingers
in this golden moment, washing
and rubbing clothes, making suds
on the surface of the water, all the time
    singing her song, lost in her own world.

You imagine touching her,
her long slender neck.
Running your fingers down her spine
squeezing her broad backside.

You imagine this, all the time
you are moving closer, and all the time
her song is running around your mind.

She bends to rinse and pull the clothes
heavy with water. Snap and crack,
rubbing and rinsing, pulling and wringing
    her hands a frenzy of activity.

Lost in her own world and her song,
you will think that this is the moment,
the right time to make your move,
to claim this beautiful woman of the water:

she who is so beautiful that
your tongue tingles in anticipation
of making contact with her smooth
coppery skin.

Within a crack and a splash,
        she will catch you around your throat.

Her green slitted eyes will hold you as her tongue
hisses, burying deep into your ear,
burrowing and tunnelling.

Now you will notice the dead fish,
the rotting things
        around the dead pet,
                amongst the rusting cans,
as you lie amongst them
                taking your last breath.

How to Explain Carnival to You

How to explain carnival to you
here and now
at day break
ready for J'Ouvert.

I'm standing with you
European settler man,
the beat half-naked,
dawn-bright between us.

I so want to tell you about carnival.
How red and blue oils on black skins
mingle with sweat as the bodies run down the hillside.
How the rhythm section is relentless
as it comes down the road again
and again. And how hands, feet, bodies,
man, woman and child cannot
stop jumping, wining, and smiling.

Instead we stand still in silence
before the hurricane
and gaze at the steel pan being loaded
onto the truck
in the half-naked beat of dawn-bright
tension as plumes of scarlet ibises
catch on a slight breeze lifting the air.

LAVENTILLE

The Map Woman

The woman's skirt is the map of the town;
along the hem runs the blue blue sea,
a constant pull onto the port,
where the silk cotton trees crowd.

Look close at the intricate detail,
like the flipped off lid of an ink-well,
splattered black lines run deep and wide,
dividing up this vibrant work of art.

Just off centre is Laventille, where
metal roof hovels crouch like crabs
in the hills. Tempers brew, sparks
fizz from the overhead electric cables.

Harsh showers send sewers and earth
swimming along the old streets,
tunnelling and burrowing
looking for home.

Desperadoes

Boots, with his close-knit, salt and pepper afro,
swings his dark muscled arms as he searches
for a 55-gallon oil drum.
Once found, with sledgehammer at the ready,
he pounds to the bottom of the drum.
They want to drive a nail in the coffin of our aspirations.

Boots works up a sweat as he expands
the metal into a dish shape.
This is sinking the pan, stretching the metal,
hammer, hammer, bang bang bang,
easing out any aggression,
as they try to drive a nail in the coffin of our aspirations.

Getting tired now, Boots does not rest.
Carrying the drum down to the beach,
he builds a fire, letting the drum burn
for just a little bit. Then plunges it, red hot,
deep into the ocean. He simmers, tempers,
making it stronger than it will ever be.

Drawing lines on the sunken head,
Boots turns the heat on and up,
as he bangs out the groove.
Like a crowd of police batons,
the outline of each note is knocked out.
They need to drive a nail in the coffin of our aspirations.

Cutting the barrel sides into a short skirt,
Boots pong pong pongs the notes in from beneath,
creating bubbles on the inside,
creating tension, making sure that they are all
vibrating at the right pitch.
They are driving a nail in the coffin of our aspirations.

With a keyboard, Boots tunes each note,
tunes each note until they sing and blend with each other.
He slaps on some bright paint; blue,
yellow or red. Dipping the whole drum
in chrome to make it shine, high shine like silver.
They will fail to drive a nail in the coffin of our aspirations.

Endure

This wasn't the way he promised it would be.
Bare floors, five to a room, babies'
faces lined with hunger, piercing
cries towards an empty oil lamp.
Love squeezes out of lives.
Boys shooting boys as regular as angel
dusting on banana leaves, long
and glistening. Violence standing
caged on corners with broken
standpipes, living next to dread.
The seething and faltering silence
as the dreamed for life
bobs on a distant horizon.
The moon is nowhere in sight.

Dirty Washing

With a rainforest in their living room
budding pods of sadness,
she is a slip of a girl
taking in people's washing.
Wearing her dress thin,
beneath an apron, like a second skin.
There is comfort in the fading pattern:
dancers on ropes, through a column of black.

Everything is just below the surface,
brewing like slightly salted, bitter coffee.
Little room to grow, swaddling fear like a corset
clocking the sky.
When there is ripping at the seams,
there'll be blood.
She'll get a second-hand report
as her hands will be wringing out
worn sheets that even when laid out
in the sun will never be white.

Trees and All

I

In front of Queen's Royal College,
under the jaundiced sun of dry
season, the poui trees
shade along the Savannah.

Standing tall their silvery-
green, palm-like leaves wave
farewell on a familiar wind,
to make room for sharp

trumpet clusters of yellow
flowers. Short-lived, everything
draws back as the promise we
never return to stains the earth.

II

In the grounds of the University,
the great old samaan tree
shelters rumours of resistance
under the hush of its canopy.

Skimming the clouds from the heavens,
stretching just as wide, its nectar,
sickly sweet, attracts
the hummingbird and parasites.

Pod, pulp, flower, root; a liquid
moon over the dripline of branches
throws growing shadows as
leaflets close together in prayer.

III

Twisting up Saddle Road,
past tiny shacks in the valley,
flame tree crowns silhouette
against the huge hanging moon.

Fern flat leaves feather,
rattling seed pods like
women's tongues gossiping
on the breeze of change.

Lava blossoms erupt, cascading
down onto Port of Spain;
rubies sparkling on a black
cloth in a hurricane.

Light from Pink Paraffin

Light from pink paraffin
holds their eyes and their bodies.
They never notice the smell
they only crave the heat.
Only later, while tucked up in bed
do they smell the burn
between the sheets
between their bodies.

PORT OF SPAIN

Mexico, 1968

'If I win, I am an American, not a black American. But if I did something bad, then they would say I am a Negro. We are black and we are proud of being black. Black America will understand what we did tonight.'
Tommie Smith (gold medallist at the 1968 Summer Olympics)

With the dust just settling on the track,
three men walk out to the podium;
two are shoeless.
In turn, each bows his head
to receive his medal;
bronze, silver and gold.

One is lynched by a black scarf.
One other, by a string of beads.
As the *Star-Spangled Banner* strikes up,
they deliver the gesture that will become
front-page news around the world.
A black-gloved fist punches the air.

Let the Niggers Burn!

After the book by Dennis Forsythe, concerning the Sir George William University Affair, Canada

Only those with a white
card can access the centre,
utilizing tomorrow's technology today.

Let a black hand try
the same and we're told a platoon
of police will aim and fire,

aim and fire. We stage a sit in.
The University is deaf to our cries.
Let them note us now.

Think of it: centuries of thinkers
erecting a monstrous fence between
a race of people and their birth-right.

We make a stand; it's labelled a riot.
We're arrested for arson.
From the cherry ashes, we rise.

The Arsonist

I love the way they dance.
It's slow at first, tantalizingly
slow, hesitant, sensual even.
Like a snake winding
to the rhythm of a magic flute.

Until they take hold.
Hold of paper, plastic, tinder,
then they're a wild frenzy
as ruby, orange and gold
lick the walls, the floor,
the tables and chairs.

I wish I could stay and watch
as they burn themselves out.
But smoke, their first cousin,
denies closeness. Smoke
extinguishes life
while flames are life.
Hot all-consuming life.

A Man Wants an Island to Love Him

You fed and nurtured me. Kept my afro
neat and my shoes clean. I took it all
with little in the way of thanks. From boiling
heat I fled, drunk on ideas, leaving
                    you weathered and redundant.

You played me the same piece of music each day.
It seeped into my blood, into my bones,
so that even away in my single bed, I dreamt
of you; your mountains, your evergreens,
                    your beat.

I returned when I could to claim your worth,
praise you, shower you with fresh dew
to then polish you to a high sheen.
There was always only ever going to be
                    you,
in my heart and soul.

My gaze is no longer obscured.
        You need me like I need you.
            Let's move and groove together
                to collect all the pieces of sky
                    for our people.

You Are Here

I
Electric cables sway over shiny and dusty vehicles sitting
bumper to bumper on hot smoking tarmac. Diesel and horns
fuming. Bright green weeds shoot through concrete; all in the
shadow of the blue-green mountains.

II
A striped red, black and white lighthouse is stranded in the
elbow of the town square.
Out of place like the white egret nesting in the brick built bus
shelter on Beecham Highway.

II
White bodies on white sheets have blue vistas under electric
air. Secured behind thick bolted gates these white burning
bodies, these white hiking up local prices for a piece of para-
dise bodies, retain a small island in their heads, even after the
vista has widened.

IV
The dew drips down green tongues, seeping into the bones of
the body lying on the ground who was once a man. Hard-
skinned feet sticking out of soiled trousers fall out of dirty flip-
flops. Matted beard matts with matted locks. Ebony eyes swim
in a yellow sea; liquid hints of egrets coming home to roost.

The Three Wives of Williams

I   Elise

You touch me in so many places,
I'm left trembling and tingling.

Yet, these feelings are marred by fear.
Without you, I prefer the nights;

the darkness all around, no moon,
is like the darkness inside of me.

All day there are others around me,
but I am alone with my emptiness.

I know you are near, by your scent –
polished mahogany, molasses, and by the heat

that creeps up my black skin
and reminds me to feel again,

the weight of your body on mine.
You have no idea how glorious

it is to be chosen by you,
to be held by you.

I have no voice to call you,
I have no right to love you.

Yet, I want to keep you.

II   Eveline

Let me have you, my little lover girl.
After I clear the earth from this garden,
only you can pass, you who have swallowed
the stars. Your lips are a chain around
my neck, as I draw birdsong from your
stomach. You who carry uprooted flowers
upon your back, poised and stylish
with their blooms.

I swim along your smooth skin, lightly
kissed by the Sun God, while the Lord
of the Night dances his darkness
into your hair. I hide within your roots.
My love for you grows deep into the forest.
I claim your legs and arms as we spin
into a single note. You supply my raft,
as we sweep into love's steep river, winding
into the sea ahead and scarlet ibises,
as bright as red flags, signal the end of the day.

III   Mayleen

She lies in their honeymoon suite, alone.
He'll be down there for years, worrying
the gap between words. The nights
are the best time for practice. She recites
the position of teeth, her training.
The darkness is not quite hers yet,
but it will become so with practice.
This gaping absence is obvious, she chooses
to be a silent partner. She rests,
face soft, listening to the tap of the large
silk cotton tree on their window, a melody
that seeps under her skin as raw as toothache.
A shudder runs down her yellow spine,
like rainy season, over and over again.

Stones

after Kapka Kassabova

They were nights of fire and brimstone.
Corner stores lost windows to stones.
At dawn, municipal workers collected glass like stones.

Who saw it coming?
Here in Trinidad, among gardenias
and steel pan, here under the bridge.

The first night, they chanted his name
                    coupled with traitor.
The second night they took their demands
                    to the sugar cane.

He sits in his big colonial house
with his hearing aid on mute;
dreaming that they march into the sea.

SUCCESS VILLAGE

What's Going On?

What's going on, son?
I see you coming, afro sky high,
fists clenched, face closed.
What's going on? Burning and looting?
For what? In my time, after the war,
where we fought and died in vain,
still used as factory fodder, we took
to the streets under Butler.
Wouldn't take a back seat in our country.
But now, what's going on? It's all fancy talk
and fancy style. African influence?
What do you know?

Father, father, I know you sit in your
broken up chair, here in the hills
and stare at nothing but wide green leaves.
You, me, everybody, is living under
the shadow of the plantations.
What's going on? Your youth has gone but
mine is here right now. You put your hope
on Williams' back. He's a white man
in a black man mask. What's going on?
I'm taking back what's mine, starting
with my mind. I'm joining hands
so we can carve up the streets.

What's going on for the first time
in my lifetime is I'm singing through
the skin of my body –
like you before me, for those
who come after we.

The Men of Success Village

They go out at night, come back early in the morning.
You hear their footsteps, the tinkling of bottles;
sudden blast of calypso music, wining of dirty mas.
Somehow you are either in bed, or at the table, waiting.

This masculine invisibility makes good of them,
a phantom of bare feet and string vests.
But when you see them, home early from the game
or at Sunday church, they are too tired,

bent, longing for rest and peace.
You hurt to see their faces, too sad or too large.
At the smell of cooking they quicken their step.
They hold their children at arms-length and chastise.

Lives wasting and smoking in the dark.

Clementine

It holds our gaze, as she rolls it – a small ginger jewel.
She says she's heard tell that rolling it first
loosens the skin, making it easier to peel.
Each roll reveals a different curve, a bright
dappled sun rolling around a sultry sky.
She uses her long thumbnail to pierce
the thick rind, then proceeds to pull back
little sections, again and again, creating
a heap of shards and leaving a reduced
version of itself behind, more yellowy

than orange and not as shiny.
It reminds me of pumpkins at Saturday market,
but smaller, much smaller. Again she uses
her pointed thumb to separate the flesh
from flesh. This is when we get to hold a piece
each. It's veiny, both dry and wet. We bite
into our portion, a squirt of juice escapes,
hitting the warm air, going to waste. Each bead
of fruit gives up its sweet treasure as we
devour a rare treat given up by a passing cart.

The Land of the Hummingbird

Light and shadow, day and night.
Three low mountains on the horizon,
an evergreen season, an unending summer
for the visitors playing mas –
a package voyage – sun, sea, rum and sex
amongst the ruins of sugar estates and forts.

The harsh music is already on the soundtrack.
Stuck in a bright green groove as we belittle ourselves
making a mess of what began, in saffron flames
and repeated with shallow faith.
Scattered by white heroes in silhouette
at the edge of the sea, we flock like pigeons
plucking at scraps of flesh,
cooing in unison, apart from the Indians.

Untitled

Even the silk cotton trees feel it.
Their white blooms, their fine sensitive veins,
bend in the breeze and beg for forgiveness
to come in a sudden shower,

and join the crowd of silence that stand
witness. One woman, held in a cell
and whipped, will never work again
in the refineries.

In the midday light, the harsh
humid light that burns hearts,
a song sweeps from mouth to mouth;
a man's memory carves out centuries.

Down and down, a calypso beat in his heart,
in an old ship that crossed an ocean;
the screams of grief – is that why
we remember certain times and not others?

The rumble of the bass, the hiss of the whip,
the seething strangled breeze.
Bruises floating through the heavy air
, like blossom and landing,

landing here, in this place.
Everything has its time. And could again.

EAST DRY RIVER

The Best of Times

Sing something simple,
on a Sunday, beamed into our small island.
We crowded around the small transistor radio
in the rumshop at the bottom of the hill,
imagining small white mouths
making melodies that came through
across the airways crystal clear
from our Mother Country
to her small, recently independent child.

We couldn't imagine the green glens
or the bubbling brooks
that Cliff Adams and his singers
sung about. But their voices
were pure and proper, voices
we rolled around our dark mouths
making the moment last,
dreaming of eventually putting
these voices into practice
in the Mother Country, with the BBC.

Sing something simple
as cares go by.
Sing something simple
just you and I.

The Den

I was nine, old enough to know where the darkness began.
Into a carved out tunnel in the mahogany hills, I crawled
with Lionel once or twice, playing dares, tight amongst
the hard parked earth.

It seemed a good idea to touch.
It seemed a good idea for our hands to explore each
dark body. In the dark knuckles knocking bone,
finger tips delving into deep dark depths.

I heard about Lionel yesterday and thought again
of our earth-packed den: the damp, dank, moist tunnel.
I could sense his long smooth limbs, his toothy white smile,
the tingles, the dark, the close, aimless dark
and the dark lost years that lay between.

Social Unrest

Today, within sound of the ocean, a man,
no longer young, is getting ready to breathe.
Before dawn, he slips out of the chattel, alone.

He has many miles to walk, too many.
The land he calls home is changing.
There is no honest way for him to make a living.

It's not what he would choose. He joins
the trail of other men walking. He is both
sorry and not sorry to share the journey.

There are many left in the town who understand this,
that the red, white and black flag is mere cloth,
see-through to where betrayal and failure lie.

Before he reaches the capital, he will take a breath.
Today is forecast hot and very close
as he is thrown into the gap, heaped and washed away.

Static Rain in Maraval

Rain waits inside us for a door to open.
Rain is heavy like full-moon lips carrying midnight.
Rain is an utterance made from broken pebbles.
Rain is that village girl who was
molested by an uncle on her way home
from school, crossing the lone cocoa hills
for a shortcut.
A variety of life and lies, looking for she –
a mahogany tipped breast
catching honey smeared raindrops. Static.
It was March, a time of blossom and damp stars.
She dripped in and out of memory for fifty years.
Rain steals everything but our secrets.

Eating a Bird

We cannot help but react
when feathers tickle skin.

There's a pull into the present
as we remember a past moment;

so risky
so thrilling,

The sensitive layer of skin
at the corner of our mouths,

our protection
our weakness,

in the painful, painful stretch
it betrays us as the beak stabs.

Before we know it, our gut
registers horror and the green
night is released.

More than we are, we yearn to fly –
yet fear our falling.

Mahoe Tree

I want to live like the mahoe tree
that sprung up on the beach last spring
and spread its heart-shaped leaves
over the moving surf.

All summer its flowers grew,
trumpeting yellows in the mornings
turning oranges to red at dusk.
Its grain carried notes

that a change was going to come.
This wild, twisted figure is steely blue.
I need to live like this mahoe tree,
solitary and ripe and free-standing

hard against the harsh winds,
and cannot be blasted away.
Keeping an eye on the far horizon
and drawing honey from the sands.

Mother to Mother

In the sun's lazy breath at day-fade,
in the seagulls' plummeting cry,
in my bulging belly and creaking joints
                    memory calls me
to the sifted flour and poured milk,
to the tossed salt over her shoulder
seeping into the current of the wind.

She bared her stomach to the full moon
to ensure that it was a boy this time.
She drank a bottle of castor oil to ease me
                    from between her legs.
She knew the hunger of green,
the words for washing away ants
and when to prepare for the time of the month.

I fit my hand along the smoothed rim of her bowl,
bind sausage meat with eggs
and I am fifteen years younger than she was
                    when she was buried.
I grow fat in the same places,
as I further work her face into mine.
I, who have never made a life without her.

Between the last and first branches of blunt buds,
between the sunlight that enters through
the kitchen window and spreads itself thin
                    as a napkin over
the shelves of peaches and pickled peppers,
I, who have many women in one body,
feel my face held between her work-worn hands.

SEA LOTS

Port of the Island

A tired ship in from the South,
crowds around the ticket barrier,
dressed in their Sunday best,
will receive no warm welcome
from the natives, no flags or banners waiting
or waving. Something about their faces
will instil a sense of fear and contempt.
A captive blue sky. Clutching their grips
they board, eager to reach the destiny
which was theirs before they were born.
Across the ocean, from one small island
to another, the future will arrive in droves.
Rivers of Blood flow behind.

The Sea is Memory

Everything in this world I have touched.
And everyone inside this world comes to me.

Each morning, my edges move back and forth,
over a culture just finding its feet.

When the shady wind bends my peaks into troughs,
I have each person's full attention.

Stand close within my constant caress
and you will not hear my roar but will be touched.

Whenever anything bad happens,
I always ask: *what have I done to deserve this?*

Why can't I behave, be ruled and
kept trapped behind glass like a freak of nature?

I sigh over the drowned souls of the Middle Passage,
their ghosts collect in my ripples looking for home.

Come to me on a moonlit night, see I was there
at the beginning and will be at the end

turning and flowing, bending and dancing before you.

Aqua Lung

Down here on the ocean floor, no air needed for breathing;
to be still is divine, life in slow motion amongst soft coral.
Above, Trinidad throbs like a taxi waiting;
down here on the ocean floor, no air needed for breathing.
Above the haunting shrieks of tourists visiting,
narrow faith heavier than a midnight cathedral.
Down here on the ocean floor, no air needed for breathing;
to be still is divine, life in slow motion amongst soft coral.

Taking people out in a small boat, I dive for a living,
the skim of my blood means I won't settle.
Trinidad sings circles around her treasures giving
away profits and fabricated images of sun, sea, and wining.
Forgotten are the ancestors of middle passing,
shallow loyalty a harsher sting than devil's nettle.
Taking people out in a small boat, I dive for a living,
The skim of my blood means I can't settle.

The Windrush Isle

The wind ramshackles the green shore for remnants of Spring,
finds only a weathered log, the bare feet of a girl –

black toes, yellow soles ploughing
the fold and waves of warm sand.

But the girl is held fast by the warm air gathering over the sea.

She imagines she sees the colonies, the lost islands rising up,
far more fascinating than daffodils and clouds in English.

Or

the letters masquerading as numbers at the bottom of her bag.

Wind, she says.
Wash over my head.
Shake my flesh to my bone.
Rattle this slackness from my head,
and stay close so that in years to come
you can blow me back,
back to those I trust will be waiting
for my return.

I will return.
To the deep moon table
in the small hilly home –
a girl no more.

And at last I will be recognised for who I am.

Can you do that for me, wind?
To me, for me, just a girl?

Blow me again and
bring me back,
another day,
another year,
another time?

The Red Cave

In the woman's cave, there are stacks
of jars with jellies, jams, pickled tomatoes

and bottles of purple-skinned plums
that look good enough to taste

their juicy sweet flesh. The walls
inside are dyed red –

scarlet, ruby, vermilion, poppy.
When she opens her cave

it's like exposing herself,
down the long cavity of deepening reds.

Air is trapped under domes of bones;
damper and warmer than the outside air.

Dark spaces breathe under the lacework
of veins. This woman feels the bubble

and burst of red each month.
Until, at last, her body swells with child.

Her cave stretches tight, billowing
with a fusion of multiplying cells.

The moonlight dyes the fields bright scarlet
leaving the thick scent of blood behind.

Fish Market

Changing from one moment to the next –
the skins of red fish – too many colours to choose.
Early morning arrives, they be
thrashing in pod nests, their eyes
fixed marbles where the sea once rode.

The men, in net vests and shorts,
stroke the fish with cool practiced passion.
And before each gleaming body,
they be on their knees claiming
their riches from the seas.

In wanting-light, small boats moored,
fish, men and sea will retreat
into the arms of women.

Spring Sea

On the pier, that Spring, he craves
the warmth of sun-bleached wood,
the stretched pier of weathered timber,
the smell of blue heat.

He wonders what the man liming by the bay
will think of him spread-eagled,
arms spread out wide,
breathing deep at the end of the pier.

Or what the woman walking the dusty streets,
singing hymns, in broken men's shoes,
will say if she sees him
in the morning of sharp Spring.

Trying to remember how to thread
chicken wire to a pole, he lies there.
Shango calling.
Fishing, raindrops and rum.

His own name sticks in his throat;
a fish bone, a stranger, a curse.
The Spring of warm wood.
He is the next generation.

The one who can leave
the island – *if I have a mind to,*
he says, to whoever will
listen.

He strokes the weathered wood,
craving splinters and deep-breathing
salt and grain, watching the sky
run cloudless, clear and blue.

BEECHAM HIGHWAY

Corbeaux

In the midday heat, they prey;
ravished and ragged with history,
their feathers midnight;
new world vultures
in an old world town.
Sewer laden waters lap the highway
where cars drive too fast for pedestrians to cross,
where these bald-headed scavengers circle
in a wave listening for the final notes
of rotting bodies, road kill and your last sleep.
Their relentless call of darkness weaves out
from their pink beaks, picking raw pink flesh
from white bones. Returning again and again
until only the past is left to drift away in the dawn.

The Bird

She is usually passed over in a crowd.
Tonight she draws the crowd.
Her palm splits into flame.
She looks at her hand and then to the crowd.
She waves her flaming hand
in slow motion above her head.
The flames travel along her arm
to her torso.
Her body is fire.
Fire is her body.
As the flames eat away her flesh
her mouth opens wide.
But there is no sound – a silent scream,
that goes on and on.
The crowd look on
not knowing what to do.
She falls at their feet.
From her back rise orange flames
until she crumples into a blackened heap.
One orange bloom glowing, dancing in their faces.

Shaddock (Pummelo)

In the mid-day heat,
at a road side vendor,
you stand up and enjoy
your first taste of shaddock.

The shape and colour
of a too large pear,
it has a smooth
cellulite dappled skin.

With a ponya,
you slice off the top and bottom,
you remove the thick outer skin
to reveal a tough white coat.

Cut it in half now, you can see
the individual compartments;
like an orange but not
like a grapefruit and not.

Taking each segment,
you peel back the thin tissue
to find full fleshy gems.
You eat them all at once,

as the sweet sticky juice
runs down your hands to your elbows.
You are left refreshed.
You are left hungry for more.

Snap

In this light, your lips open
like red poinsettia; a firework in your face.
Weird things always happen to our people.
We stalk agouti, glide towards them in the orange light
far above the capital. We go to speak the same verb.

In this light, the streets are haunting, sacred.
The green cedars guard the warriors
like protective parents.
We start to say that we wouldn't mind dying here.
Like the scarlet ibis flocking at dusk
squealing out the final harsh calls of our heritage.

Far From Delhi

Soon, I will be as wise as a swami by the Ganges.
Soon, they will come to the borders of Caroni.

As the morning's gauzy humidity burns away, light
will splinter the low evergreen fields of sugar cane and rice.

With the air pungent with tamarind and cumin,
they will struggle to concoct one flame with our deyas.

Still, my people will walk the worn road balancing clay
pots on our heads, as cows and chickens wander unchecked.

'The Long March'

12 March 1970, the March to Caroni by Black Power revolutionaries led by the National Joint Action Committee (NJAC)

Arm in arm ten thousand strong,
disciplined and silent,
with the Northern Range on their backs
they start the long hot trek
down the old Southern Main Road.

The silent, uneasy, undulating
Caroni plains lie out ahead.
Rumour circulates that the glistening
green cane swaying in the breeze
holds men, armed and waiting.

Deep into their territory, young Indian
men and women welcome the crowd
with applause, water and juice. Elders stay
watching from a distance as rumour runs
before them; black men coming to rape their women.

In the billowing cane, the sweltering
heat, the crowd reach Chaguanas,
peacefully. Africans and Indians unite.
With night coming on and people exhausted,
this is an historic day, an historic moment.

A Different Shade of Red

This evening the weather broke
and threatening light
brought into the long night,

the fire you
carried for years
poured into me.

From your naked flesh
came the fossilised song
of a hummingbird.

Then your words,
a heavy palette, raining all day
onto the surface of my skin,

intensified with the repetition
of rain on rain. You'll bring me
another colour next time, deeper

ruby, you once held for a moment
before the water broke
and threatening light

as you dived again into the long night
as birds slipped
and motioned distress.

MORVANT

Before Dawn on Lady Young Road

And the breeze bears along as well,
from down by the port,
when the tide's just so,
when the sewerage is just so.
The metallic residue of old refineries,
the rotting wharves and peeling lighthouse,
vicious asphalt, nutty cacao, burnt rice,
ethanol from the sugar mills.

A soup of oil, sweat and blood
trailing fifty years
seeping through the dusty red earth, the odour
almost comforting by now, like food,
wafting through Success Village.
With its fevers and dreams,
barefoot generations breathing together,
doors left open in case some soul cries.

My Daughter Sleeping in April

I love the smell of my daughter sleeping,
cuddled in tight to my side,
especially in the early hours with the coming light.
Surprising and fresh, the room warming
and so many birds, so many tunes.
The downy light touches her head,
her body untangles along the length of my arm;
she is dreaming of milk, colours and sleep.
I touch her cheek, my baby,
who can hardly see me yet, so I lower my face.
I hang with the air, like a sigh breaking
as she breathes deeply and the morning purrs.

Flip-flop

He tucks his feet into yellow plastic flip-flops
and flaps out onto the veranda.
From the front room, with its glass cabinet
and artificial egrets on the wall,
she can see his head bobbing.

Years ago, he promised to take her to New York.
He was gorgeous and kind then, a dove,
even when the pulse of life could be seen
throbbing through his wiry frame.

The dusk rises and blurs like a cloud.
She stands by the refrigerator,
rusted and blackened with age.
Regret hums in the air like electricity.

Basil Davis, the First Martyr

9 April 1970

Gun shots pierce the heat
stagnant over Woodford Square.

The street seeps red.
Feelings flood red.
His coffin clothed in red.

With berets perched on Afros,
thousands strong we march.
We were betrayed.

Black man in power does not
signify Black Power.

Still Life

after Sharon Olds

At moments, I almost thought of him.
I was wandering through the market
when he was shot.

I was with dappled shaddock. I was in
the vicinity of rough yams, of floppy
green dasheen and firm breadfruits.

Juicy red bell peppers – and wilted stalks –
he was wading into a sea of sweaty bodies,
lapping onto Woodford Square,

casting off his silence, while I was wandering
crates of coconuts, with broken heads
and milk drying. Seeds of a watermelon

dripped along the dusty tracks.
He had settled me from the start, to food,
he cried out in pain, to the wholeness

of stew, how it stood in for that spirit
of home. The mixture of lamb, onions,
tomatoes, curry powder and cumin, trailing

scents through the Parish, hot and thick.
And my son was a moving boat, a touring heat,
he stood shoulder to shoulder with his brothers

and demanded to keep his island his own.
He raised his fist into his chest and held
it there and screamed, and fell to the pavement.

And I wandered, calm, amongst the beheaded
red snapper, and crabs, clams, silver prawns
and sword fish, even sharp tooth shark,

strung up by its tail like a wide sail.
There are things I will never know about a mother's love.
I wandered, ignorant to my son, among

the sweet potatoes, marrows with their holy
stripes. He lay there and I walked blind
through the waves.

The Last Four Lines for Basil Davis

after Gwendolyn Brooks

after the killing
after the burial

Basil's mother is a weary-faced thing;
                    the trace of stretched pitch.
She sits in a black room,
                    drinking white rum.
She kisses her murdered boy,
                    and she is pitiful.
Chaos in swirling greys
                    through this red island.

Red Template

Witness the ibises coming home at dusk,
bright as red banners,
in a light the colour of metal.

Red coming home to rest in the swampy Caroni plains,
beaks shaded under cabbage palms,
feet spread into a blue river underneath brown.

The air is dense with sewage and rumour.
Across the way, flapping like the red birds,
flapping like strange birds migrating,

flapping like some bird smelling danger in the air,
she wakes from a possessed sleep
and stares with eyes full of apologies.

She feels the friction of lost years
running through her hands like nettles,
tastes globes of spice on her tongue.

A fragile silence broken by bone beaten on a drum.

After the Strike

after Sîan Hughes

This is a seamless change, and I will learn
to go back into the home without screaming.
It is only right to find myself alone
all day. It is only right to keep quiet
and for no one to know my thoughts. I will adjust.

Already I have gotten used to the sound of my thoughts
squealing around in my head day after day.
It is almost like being empty to me, almost
like the days themselves. I will learn
to close the door, turn aside and breathe.

The Last Lap

In the country's hospital bed, late at night,
her body waits to be claimed.
Her soul sits beside it on a plastic chair,
no one comes to give her life again.

Think of her body, always lonely.
At night prowling the streets,
a shadow, creeping and crawling
such a long distance.

And already she is forgotten,
no pause out of respect,
the name tag at the bottom of her
bed already erased.

Barely a ripple in death as in life.

Flamingo Lilies

Her favourite were flamingo lilies. Pink flames.
I try to get them with the buds still closed
like pursed pink lips attempting to keep quiet.
In time, they can be coaxed open, open to reveal
pale pink tips pointing from a centre
of deep, deep fleshy pink.

She only received flamingo lilies on special occasions;
birthdays, Mother's Day, Christmas Eve.
Now whenever I visit I bring them.
Sharp pink, heart-shaped heads bobbing
on soft green stems. They are easy to arrange,
shades of marshmallow pink nodding
against granite stone. Pink tongues
whispering *I love you* once more.

at the city centre here
in this green square
the stone men closed
and the trees stand witness
that men do not die
but grow in dreams of generations
bitter and beautiful as cedar leaves

Eric Roach, 'City Centre 70'